Creating**MAGIC**

Ed Ackerley, M.Ed.

This book is designed to share with readers insights about creativity with personal stories and anecdotes gained by the author, Edward E. Ackerley, in over twenty-five years as an advertising agency principal and over a decade of college teaching.

CreatingMAGIC helps you learn skills to enhance your life with Creativity! This companion book to the popular creative seminar is a simple selection of stories revealing profound truths about creativity.

Using real life examples from life and business, the book is a quick read for all ages, and can give anyone who reads it a new perspective on creativity and how it affects personal change, interpersonal relationships, business and success.

For more information contact the author at:

PHONE: 520.850.7058
EMAIL: DoctorMAGIC27622@aol.com

 Copyright © 2002 E.T. NEDDER Publishing
All rights reserved.

Additional copies of this publication may be purchased by sending check or money order for $15.95 plus $4.00 postage and handling to: E.T. NEDDER Publishing, PMB #299, 9121 East Tanque Verde, STE #105, Tucson, Arizona 85749-8390. Or call toll free 1-877-817-2742. Fax: 1-520-760-5883. www.NEDDERPublishing.com.

ISBN 1-893757-24-2 Order #24-2

10 9 8 7 6 5 4 3 2

Table of Contents

INTRODUCTION

Creating**MAGIC**! The creativity of the human spirit and the power of human thought is fascinating. This book is about how to become more creative. Creativity is one of the most important skills we can possess because through it we can enhance our own personal lives, our interpersonal relationships and can use creativity to advance our careers, our dreams and aspirations.

Creating**MAGIC** happened because the subject has become a part of my professional life and came about through researching creativity for my doctoral dissertation. I also enjoy teaching people how to unleash their creative power and to use it to unlock their creativity. The companion seminar which I present entitled Creating**MAGIC** helps people come to realize how very important creativity is in our lives.

You can become more creative and you can use creativity to make your life magical. This book will present several skills to start you on the road to a more creative and inspired life. Perhaps you too can use this information to make your life more enhanced each day.

This book is dedicated to my wife Susan whose encouragement has helped me fulfill my dreams...and to our sons Kyle, Kevin and Kasey. Their creative magic is what inspires me each and every day.

Ed Ackerley, M.Ed.

CHAPTER 1

ALLEY HOPPING

For my tenth birthday, my parents' gift to me was the ultimate for a young boy . . . a black Schwinn bicycle. It was as awesome and came complete with white decal racing stripes. This bike was the best gift I had ever received and gave me instant freedom.

The bicycle had a way of calling me from the backyard. Almost every morning during the summer of 1968, I would explore the alleys of my youth, bordered by the streets of my neighborhood.

My brother and I rode down these endless alleys and gathered the castaways of of middle income life . . . bricks, wood and other discards. We needed these materials to build our clubhouse which we fondly referred to as a "fort". We called this ambitious activity "Alley Hopping."

We dug a giant hole in the backyard . . . enclosed it with wood and built our fort two stories high. That summer, we would work all day gathering materials and building our fort, and after dinner would sit inside and marvel at our creation. We were "banditos" and this was our hideaway.

Think back to your memories of your own childhood. Do you remember the creative spirit of your youth? Perhaps acting out the fantasy of make believe and your ability to invent? Did you ever play house, army, doctor, postman or cowboys and Indians? Did you ever imitate tv or movie characters and superheros?

One of my sons used to wear a superhero cape. It was part of a Halloween costume, but he adopted it as part of his persona. During a three month period of his young life, when he would wear the cape he *was* that superhero. He wore the cape all day long, at daycare, during dinner, even to bed. That cape was his key to saving the world as the greatest superhero of all time.

Creativity is important to a fulfilled life, yet as we grow older we tend to inhibit the creative process. It seems we consciously stifle the creative magic we had as children.

Developing skills remains an important cornerstone of many personal development programs. When leadership lists were developed many included traits like: Problem Analysis, Discernment, Judgement, Integrity, Vulnerability, Organizational Ability, Decisiveness, Sensitivity, Awareness of the Human Spirit, Stress Tolerance, Oral and Written Communication, Courage in Relationships, Sense of Humor, Range of Interest, Personal Motivation, Historical Perspective, Education and more. At the turn of the century, an effort was made to update these lists to include Setting Direction, Teamwork, Results Orientation, Development of Others and Understanding Own Strengths and Weaknesses. Conspicuously missing from most personal skills lists is *Creativity*.

Why is *Creativity* so critically needed in your life? You most likely have "lost" the creativity of your youth if you are like the majority of adults. Perhaps your creativity has changed since you began formal schooling and rules. You were undoubtedly told when you were young to conform and *color inside the lines*.

Although a "process", skills relating to creativity can enhance your personal relationships. This important personal skill is very powerful in the success of a good leader. As children, our creativity manifests itself through play. Creativity takes a secondary position behind skills of the classroom as we enter formal education. We are taught to "color within the lines" and to look at life objectively, factually and develop good study and learning habits.

As we progress through secondary education, creativity begins to manifest itself through the performing and visual arts while we tend to lose the unbridled creativity that we once had as children. Many researchers argue that creativity is not necessarily being stifled, but other equally important life skills are being taught and rehearsed, causing creativity to become less prominent. The purpose of this book is to help you recapture the creativity of your youth.

One question I ask in CreatingMagic seminars is "How would you describe the color of creativity?"

Some say RED because red symbolizes the passion and emotion of being human. Others say BLUE representing the cleansing of water and the breath of life. Some suggest GREEN symbolizing growth and creation. Still others offer YELLOW symbolizing sunshine and the flame of inspiration.

Many times the response is the RAINBOW of colors as we focus on the total array of human gifts. But perhaps the best color which represents creativity is not really very glamorous and perhaps somewhat forbidding: GRAY. Gray represents something we all have, but do not use to its potential . . . our human mind.

Creativity has been defined as an individual taking two disconnected ideas and putting them together to form something new and exciting. As human beings, we have a magical power of creating something new simply by thinking it. We have the power to ask "why?" and "why not?".

Creativity begins in our thoughts and ideas. Our brains have a phenomenal unmatched power that when unleashed can send forth an ocean from a simple idea.

In business consulting, this "alley hopping" concept is used regularly. As human beings, we tend to be very judgmental and approach new ideas with skepticism. Using a creative technique called "Brainstorming" . . . key players come together and begin to make lists of ideas. They are instructed to not cast judgement on the ideas, but rather accomplish the task of writing down as many ideas related to the topic as they can in a reasonable amount of time. Mentally, each participant is walking down the alleys of their life experience and bringing forth previously discarded information as something new. Someone is designated as the "scribe," objectively transcribing and lists the ideas. Through a process of organized and focussed evaluation the group begins to isolate the ideas which seem to make the most sense for the overall objectives. If you travel down the corridors of your mind and collect the ideas, and combine them to make something new, you are "alley hopping" and finding the treasures which spawn creativity.

Creativity is best accomplished when we change our point of view. The play of your youth was a manifestation of the power of your mind's ability to create with thought, sound, and emotion. This ability allowed you to break through the barriers of everyday life and focus on simple big ideas.

To accomplish this same free spirit of creativity as an adult, it is important to change your frame of reference.

Think of it this way. Your life is much like a a story (and if you are fortunate a fairy tale). It has a beginning, a middle and an end. Hopefully, it also has purpose. Throughout your life you gain experience and are exposed to many different viewpoints and opinions . . . and your mind is like a sponge absorbing your experiences in the recesses of your mind.

The problem with most adults is the inability to use this story to create something new and exciting. The first creative suggestion will be to take an inventory of how you are already demonstrating creativity in your life:

CREATIVE BENCHMARK

Make a list of all the things you CAN DO that are creative. This might be a talent for music, art, communicating, or a craft, hobby or even things from your profession.

Your list should contain at least twelve ways you are creative:

Both in your personal life, and your business life, it is important to go "alley hopping" in your mind and in your experiences to find the discards of your life. Much like the memories of your childhood, within the recesses of your mind you can find the basis of a new, refreshing creative outlook. As a child you were instructed to "color inside the lines" and to tame your creative instincts . . . and through CreatingMagic we hope to teach you how to unleash these ideas. Try not to inhibit your creative instincts, but to enhance your creativity. As we grow our societal instincts are to conform and "fit in". But it is through creativity that we can enhance our life and those around us.

Try the skill of brainstorming the next time you face a challenge in your life that seems insurmountable. Use this process to help change your point of view and go "alley hopping" and find some discards that you can turn into something valuable.

In the coming chapters, you will learn the skills to unleash the power of creativity within you. The story of your life started with a creative beginning . . . and perhaps now you, like most adults, are at a stage where creativity may not be as important as it once was. Together we will go "alley hopping" to find treasures to build your creativity. A great skill to learn is the little phrase of a small engine that could . . . positive thought . . . .*I CAN*. You *can* be creative, you *can* be more creative, you *can* learn the skills and your life will become enhanced.

CHAPTER 2

A TUNE IN A BUCKET

The move from the unbridled creativity of young children to the stifled concepts we display as adults comes with a price. We tend to lose our "creative spontaneity" we had when we were young. As this transformation takes place, we can rearrange our priorities to become more childlike and continue to absorb the wonder of the world well into our life. Adults see themselves often as "not very creative." See if you can relate to one of these types of creatives:

BUCKETS — These are the people when asked "can you sing?" quickly respond with "I can't even carry a tune in a bucket." As an adult, they see themselves as outwardly totally "uncreative" and that they lack the basic qualities to perform, draw, construct or create anything that might be considered artistic. They spend most of their life defending the fact that they can not do what they see others do. In most cases, they have given up on their potential for learning something creative or something artistic.

DABBLERS — These are the people who when asked "can you sing, dance or draw?" often respond with, "well, I took lessons when I was a child and I can play a couple of tunes on the piano" . . . or "I used to doodle quite a bit in class and got pretty good at cartoon figures but I never really followed up on my talents." These are the people who blossom when in a unique setting like a party, where if they are coerced into performance may show a sample of their talents (like playing a tune on the piano, doing a magic trick, or telling a story.) However, most of the time, they revert to not wanting to practice the creative form with which they might have some propensity, yet at the same time they recognize that the might have a little talent and show it from time to time.

BEHOLDERS — These are the people who think they are creative, yet those who are around them disagree. These are the people that say, "Yes, I can sing" . . . and they muster the courage to sing karaoke at a party . . . and they barge ahead with limited inhibitions and belt out a song, or two, or a dozen (depending on how many drinks they have had). Their idea of creativity is to just do it. These are the people who practice their craft on a regular basis (like telling jokes, writing down new jokes on an old piece of paper and saving it in their wallet for just the perfect time when they can pull it out and begin to tell jokes to a new audience). This type of person usually thinks they are creative, but this definitely is in the eye of the beholder.

AMAZERS — These are the people who can sing, they can dance, they can draw, they can perform . . . but they very often do not broadcast this, even to those they know well. Their innate talents are often hidden from those who are closest to them (especially friends and peers) and when they are discovered people are "amazed" at the quality of the talent these people possess. Many times the amazers are tied to jobs where creative thinking and implementation are the keys to success (people jobs, relationship building, something new everyday) however many of the amazers are the engineer/linear thinking types who happen to have a latent talent.

NATURALS — These are the people all creatives wish they could be. They simply have the ability to draw, sing, perform, paint, produce, create. For these, using their creative ability is second nature and comes easy. They are not "pompous" with their talents, they simply know that their craft, their abilities, and their talents are gifts they have . . . and they use them and exploit them to please family, friends and co-workers.

Many of us move from NATURALS as children to BUCKETS. To move beyond being a bucket, you must unleash the creative power you possess.

CHAPTER 3

THE STORY

Telling a story is probably as old as humans. Long before there was written language or television or the internet, people probably sat around making up and telling stories. Tribes and clans told stories to explain natural phenomena to their children or to endow their culture with tradition and history. Most likely, stories served as a form of entertainment to many.

Think back in your own life and the "story" it brings forth about your existence and your experiences. As children, most of us created stories which we acted out as a form of play. People take their stories with them throughout their life. And these stories change each time they are told as the meaningful parts are enhanced and the not so meaningful parts are dropped. Stories change as they are handed down from one generation to another. But stories provide insight, engagement and a visual picture easy enough for most to readily understand.

Perhaps one of the greatest stories ever told in philosophy is by Socrates in Plato's *Republic*. It is the analogy entitled **Allegory of the Cave** and outlines Plato's sense of how people think and how they pursue knowledge.

The **Allegory of the Cave** is about a place underground where prisoners have been chained since childhood. With their heads fastened in such a way so they cannot see what is behind them, only what is in front of them. The only thing they know would be the reflected shadow and voices coming from the cave wall in front of them. When one prisoner is allowed to turn around, he will be fascinated by the fire behind him creating the shadows on the wall. If he is allowed to go into the sunlight, although frightening for him, he will see things never seen before. If he comes back and tries to tell the prisoners of what he saw, he would be a different person and would have a hard time convincing them of the life beyond the cave.

Plato uses this story to describe the differences between what we believe and what we know. The prisoners in the chained position see themselves and their world and believe the shadows on the wall are real, yet when the prisoner returns to tell them about sunlight, it is difficult for the rest to understand. Plato, through Socrates, describes this as part of the training for the leaders of the Republic which he is building through philosophy . . . and Plato accomplishes this through eloquently telling a story.

Socrates tells of the enlightenment of the people in the cave based on their new viewpoint which is fascinating in its simplicity, yet so very powerful in meaning. Plato takes a simple analogy and wraps it into such a great story.

One of the pioneers in modern thinking was the English philosopher John Locke whose work includes *Some Thoughts Concerning Education* written in 1693. In his writing throughout his life he stressed the theory that the human mind starts as a blank sheet of paper.

The mind has no inborn ideas, but throughout life it forms its ideas only from impressions (experiences which can be told in stories) that are written on this blank page.

Locke presents to us the blank page on which the story of education, of knowledge, natural and physical experiences are written as we live out our life in a story. In this we can find creativity as a process of skill development.

Some 2,500 years after Plato wrote *The Republic*, storytelling continues to be a resource for unleashing creativity and is so important to the growth and learning of children and how they are creative and live out this creativity instinctively. A child learns and develops from relative primitive knowledge to the adult who has depth and breadth of knowledge. But children do know many things, much of it creative in scope and wonder.

Children can learn a lot from a story. Stories have a natural rhythm and a logical progression from a point or place in time an ending, usually "happy."

The telling of a *story* is captivating. It is ever so simple and understandable to even a young child, but carries with it a powerful message. The story is a unique way to communicate that which is difficult to relate, because a storyteller can share information in a way that is memorable and engaging. When a good story is disclosed, like Plato's **Allegory of the Cave**, the human mind seems to remember this long after the words have gone away. Like ink on a blank page as Locke espouses, the story turns into vision and is lodged in the long term memory.

You too have a story which is played out in a simple but powerful way everyday. Our challenge is to see if we can capture this story so your creativity can shine.

CHAPTER 4

CHANGE THE PARADIGM

In CreatingMagic seminars, I conduct an activity which supports the theory that adults try to color inside the lines. All the years of formal education seem to pay off as demonstrated by the opening creative assignment. Here is the exercise:

At the beginning of the seminar I place a piece of paper in a folder in front of each attendee along with several large felt tip markers. The paper has a "frame" on one side . . . complete with an ornate border . . . which is reminiscent of a frame of an old-fashioned portrait.

During the presentation I draw attention to the supplies and give the following instructions:

"In your CreatingMagic folder in front of you, there is a piece of paper with a frame on it. And there are some markers on the tables as well. As we start this journey of creativity, I would ask you to please draw a portrait of yourself. You will have a couple of minutes to draw your picture."

After all have completed the drawings, they are asked to hold them up for the rest of the participants to see. The overwhelming majority draw a picture on the side of the paper with the frame. In fact, in all of the years of this experiment, not one person has drawn on the reverse side of the paper. Other trends include: most draw in a vertical or portrait style; many draw a smiley face; and to be adventurous, many include a little stick figure body.

Never has anyone drawn a portrait as they were as a baby or project their life twenty-five years hence. The pictures are consistent from seminar to seminar.

What does this simple demonstration mean? First, without any prompting participants "do what they are told" because of their social conditioning. They draw a portrait of themselves because of the instructions given . . . and in that regard they assume that the drawing needs to be on the side of the paper with the frame and a reflection of life at that very moment.

When we conform to rules or instructions because of habit or social conditioning, we inhibit our creativity. Here are questions which might demonstrate this principal in your own life: Do you drive to work via the same route, shop in the same stores and eat in the same restaurants, watch the same television programs and develop the same routines?

Human habits help us perform tasks more efficiently. Although this provides efficiency, at times it is at the cost of creativity. Begin to break these rules to be creative.

The ability to transform your view to a new perspective . . . that of the simple but big ideas of a child . . . .helps unleash creative thought. To become more creative, rekindle the creativity of your childhood, because in order to be "creative" you need to look at the world through a new viewpoint, a simple view.

To be successful, you must open your mind to other views and change the perspective of the way you see things. A successful business views the situation as their customers do. This is called **changing the paradigm**.

A paradigm is derived from the Greek word *paradigma*, meaning pattern or example. In his book *The Structure of Scientific Revolutions*, Thomas Kuhn argued that all 'normal science' takes place within a pattern or paradigm and that revolutions in scientific thought only come about when people are able to break out of the pattern and create new ways of seeing and thinking – a new paradigm.

Kuhn, Thomas, The Structure of Scientific Revolutions (University of Chicago Press, 1996)

In a view of radical change, Kuhn said: "Individuals who break through by inventing a new paradigm are almost always . . . either very young or very new to the field whose paradigm they change . . . . these are the men who, being little committed by prior practice to the traditional rules of normal science, are particularly likely to see that those rules no longer define a playable game and to conceive another set that can replace them."

A workable definition of a paradigm is a set of values agreed to by a particular society which frames a common vision of reality for that group.

Changing your perspective or "changing the paradigm" is important. In the classes I teach at the University of Arizona I often share this letter with students near the end of the semester . . . many of them are seniors ready to graduate:

Dear Mom and Dad:

Since it is getting close to the end of the year I thought I would write you a note and let you know how I am doing. These last few weeks have been hectic. I have had so much to do, and so much school work. School has been hard. I have an early advertising class and it's been difficult to wake to get to class on time.

Many times I arrive late. I think I am going to get a C in this class. It really doesn't matter, because I have switched majors from Business to History of Art. You always have told me to follow my dream, so I have. It is a little late, but it is fun watching the models they pay strip naked and stand there for hours while we all draw them. Drawing the naked human body is such a rush. I'm not very good at it, but I've seen a lot of things I didn't see in high school! One of my art professors is really cool . . . his name is Dan and I am in love with him.

He introduced me to some erotic paintings and ever since I have just adored him. We've taken a lot of bike trips lately . . . it is so fun travelling down the back roads of Arizona on a Harley! Although we have not had a lot of money I have been working some at an adult entertainment club . . . because I have been using the credit card to buy food and it will be maxed out in another week. By the way, you can reach me at a new address. I have moved out of the sorority and I have moved in with Dan and his brother, Charlie. Although it's a one bedroom apartment, we find it to be very cozy . . . and with our hectic schedules we just share the bed. Oh, I forgot to tell you that we think we are pregnant. Dan and Charlie will make such good fathers as we are not really sure at this point which one is the dad. And although I have cut back on the drugs, the doctor says a little red wine won't hurt the twins. You will make wonderful grandparents. Well, I have to study now for my advertising final . . .

By the way . . . I have not changed majors, I still live in the sorority, I have not met a teacher named Dan or his brother, I am not pregnant with twins and I have not been using drugs. I am the same little girl that daddy dropped off at campus four years ago. I have grown up a lot Although I am getting a C in my advertising class, I am sure you realize now what that means in perspective. I love you. Send money.

Your loving daughter.

LISTEN. Creativity starts when you change your point of view. Established patterns and habits guide us through everyday life and provide comfort but block the view of the world. Changing the paradigm, to search for the simple yet big idea, is to transform the way you see the world . . . that is how you become more CREATIVE. Like the daughter points out to her parents, changing your perspective can make a big difference. Here are some practical examples of changing perspective:

• When you return home after a long day, get down on the floor and play with your child at their level, not from your chair.

• While at your desk at work, stand up to talk on the phone, you will soon discover that chatter wastes a lot of time.

- Drive to work via a different route everyday for a week.

- Write a love letter by sitting in the dark and recording it on a recorder.

- Change the names of common things: Paying personal bills to "investments in my family"; stress to "positive pressure"; mundane household chores to "my personal contribution to our lifestyle"; studying for a test to "increasing my knowledge of the subject".

- Walk toward things that you fear, do not retreat.

- Look at life as an opportunity to enjoy creation.

For over thirty years, my family's advertising agency was housed in a building in the center of town. When my father opened the agency in 1968, the building was a nice mid-town complex next to a restaurant that many people frequented. Throughout the years, our clients, the media and suppliers came to know us because of that building.

During the time we were in that building, we grew from one ten foot by ten foot office to a window front office with nine different rooms and lots of space. As we grew, we continued to store client commercials, scripts, paperwork, purchase orders and more. As chance would have it, we moved after thirty years. The change of venues brought new computers, work stations, upgraded facilities. Indeed, it brought to all of us a new focus on our business. We eliminated thousands of unneeded documents, discarded the old ways and had to learn new ways, and computerized our systems, many of which had been manual for decades.

In making this change of location, and an internal change in perspective, our client base shifted from small retail stores to a more lucrative travel industry base. Our clients and media began to view us not as an old agency,but a hot shop with a great new look.

Certainly, I am not suggesting you change offices, but the exercise is a physical reminder of what it means to "change the paradigm" and to force yourself to focus on a new viewpoint. It is somewhat akin to changing the layout of your living room or bedroom to create a new look or spice up your life.

In the coming week, when you are asked to perform a task try something different. Try to look at it from the viewpoint of the person asking you to assist with the task. Is there a way you can look at this situation from their point of view? Although tempting, try not to jump at the first and most logical or traditional solution. Add some newness to your life on an ongoing basis and you will begin to see creativity come alive. Break a rule or create a new rule. Focus on changing the paradigm. Creative people are always looking for new ways to stir things up in a way that the paradigm shifts. Take a refreshing look at your life, and you will see some opportunity to change the paradigm.

CHAPTER 5

THE BIG IDEA

Thousands of people come to the southwestern United States every year because of the weather. The climate is temperate during the winter and although hot during the summer *"it's a dry heat"*. Along with the throngs of winter visitors come hundreds of homeless men and women who try to escape the harsh climates of the north.

Many of these homeless have taken to the street corners to solicit commuters for money. The art of begging has come a long way and this phenomena is proof. Recently, I saw a man who was disheveled and dirty standing on a corner with a sign. He most likely had all of his worldly possessions bundled inside his sleeping bag. He was no different than the countless others who call the concrete traffic islands home during the day and the arroyos and parks their beds at night. Their modus operandi is the same..they hold a sign and beg for any spare change passers-by can muster. The signs are consistent . . . made of old cardboard boxes with with messages scrawled like:

Out of work. Three kids. Anything. Pleaz Help. God Bless

But on this day, this character was different. His sign read:

It worked. The sign made you think and take notice. Countless motorists rolled down their windows and shared spare change with him. He was vibrant and resourceful, he smiled a lot, and many rewarded him.

One day I was driving with my two youngest boys when we came upon one of this homeless man holding the sign and begging for money. One of the boys asked "Dad, what is that man doing?"

In a moment of flippant response I said that he was asking for money so that he could "afford his condo on Maui." It was a rather caustic response and reflected the general ambivalence I had for these people who had come to my hometown from all over the country to ask *me* for money.

In my own way, I was poor and I needed more resources too . . . and I regarded these homeless as scavengers invading my civic comfort zone. It seemed they were everywhere, on every corner, and after a while I simply ignored them as if they were not there.

The reply from the back seat was, "really?"

At that moment I knew I had a genuine teaching opportunity with them and I dug down deep into my fatherliness and responded:

"Well boys, that man is probably homeless. He does not have enough money for a house like we have, or for that matter he probably has not eaten in some time. He most likely does not have a family or a job and if he did he either lost them because he got sick or something happened. He is just asking people for help . . . and what he needs most is money to get something to eat to make it through the night."

There was complete silence.

About thirty-seconds later there was a small but deliberate voice from the back. Innocent in understanding but powerful in its simplicity, one of my sons said: "Dad, can we give him some money?" We rolled down the window and handed the man our change and I have never since seen these men and women in the same light . . . and many times have shared what I have with them. This powerful perspective of my own children really moved me.

There are other perspectives on how to help the homeless, and many argue that giving money to people who ask for it on a corner may not be the best for them and for their well being. Experts suggest supporting your favorite charity or social agency to help deal with these situations. However, in this perspective, the cost of a few cents made a powerful impact on me and my sons, one that I will never forget.

There probably is no greater source of creative power than to unleash human emotions . . . .humor, sadness, love, loneliness, joy, happiness, and more. The compassion my boys showed for this homeless man translated into a critical change in my viewpoint. It is this connectedness with each other that drives the POWER OF CREATIVITY.

One of the precepts of good communication is to strip away the fluff to get to the point. If that point has universal appeal, with each person who sees it identifying it in their own emotional way, then the communication can connect on an important level. This is the challenge of modern advertising . . . conveying a message about products, services and ideas on an emotional level which brings us together in simple and common understanding.

The difficulty in constructing communication is perspective. What you think is funny the next person may not. What you think is crazy, dumb, exciting, engaging, unrealistic, etc. may not be the same as the next person. The ability to craft advertisements that unite us in our common understanding with powerful images in a simple context is the constant challenge of advertising creative directors.

LISTEN. You can begin to become creative when you tap into your humanness, the child within, by creating ideas that focus on emotion and stir the senses.

To do this, separate yourself from your own perspective. You need to detach yourself in order to see a new view much like I had indifference to the homeless prior to the question my sons posed. This changing of the paradigm is vitally important.

Over the years our company has represented a blue-chip list of clients in retail, tourism and more recently the hotel industry. We challenge our clients to unleash their creativity and connect emotionally with their customers through a concept called the "big idea."

The big idea was first defined by David Olgilvy and others in the sixties and described the flash of genius or burst of inspiration that captures the essence of the communication in an understandable, engaging concept. The big idea is also defined in the halls of our agency by these key words which happen to be part of our creative motto: simplicity, clarity, and quality. Capturing that simple big idea in advertising is Creativity.

Each year television commercials debut on programs with high ratings with the most famous being the Superbowl. Take notice next time. The majority of these award winning ads are those that are simple.

You probably have a favorite TV commercial . . . think about it, the concept is probably very simple, one with which you can relate easily and so can a grandmother as well as a five year old.

For over one hundred years, Sears Roebuck and Company sold soft goods, clothing, apparel, household items, and hardlines including washing machines, dryers, television, vacuums, car batteries and more. As a store molded in the traditional format of a department store, Sears was a mainstay in American commerce in the 1900s. However, in the last part of the century, Sears was still holding on to its past. Known for large stores selling everything for the home, they sold millions of dollars of merchandise to people in the midwest and across the country through their famous Sears catalog. I recall my mom buying me and my brothers and sisters shoes through the catalog.

Sears had enjoyed years of being the number one retailer in the world . . . and then things began to change. Due to competition from other retailers, and new and faster distribution techniques, stores like Wal-Mart began to overtake Sears dominance.

Sears had other complications. Its Discover Card Services were spun off, its lifetime guarantee on DieHard batteries continued to drain resources, its affiliation with Allstate was in question after some devastating hurricanes in the southeast and Sears core customer, the middle-aged modern housewife, was being lured away by the intense competition.

Sears executives had to make some very important decisions about the future of its stores. One of the first radical changes was to cease publication of its catalog and to some degree replace it with Sears.com.

Decisions were also made about the mix of products offered for sale in their stores.

Working with their advertising agency, they embarked on a stunning and significant "retooling" of the traditional Sears image to change the paradigm. Sears would maintain its dominance only by getting back to basics, reducing its products and concentrating on what got them to number one in the first place.

Enter one of the greatest repositioning advertising campaigns in history . . . you know it *"Come See The Softer Side of Sears!"* This campaign reintroduced their primary target market – today's modern housewife, (who had left the farmhouse and now was working equally in the marketplace from nine to five) to the softer side of Sears. It was fashion merchandise that would become the focus.

"The Softer Side of Sears" was a revolutionary "big idea" that has helped Sears rebound and stay competitive. Other companies employ this big idea concept which is evidenced by their use of similar campaigns to seek out the big idea and communicate it to their customers.What they are really doing is connecting with their very important best customers on

an emotional level that brings personality to the some-times sterile seller/buyer relationship.

CREATIVE BENCHMARK

In the CreatingMagic seminar, participants are asked to create a Big Idea bumper sticker that tells their most important quality to anyone who sees it . Using just seven or less words, how do you see your-self? When I did this to describe me, I came up with:

HOT! HOT! HOT!

In the space below, make a big idea bumper sticker for you:

```
┌──────────────────────────────────────────┐
│                                          │
│                                          │
│                                          │
│                                          │
│                                          │
└──────────────────────────────────────────┘
```

There are times in your life when a small child, a family celebration, a business transition, or some other special event will trigger an "epiphany" within you. Like the teaching moment I had with my small boys in giving to the homeless man, or the realization that Sears had with the prospect of losing their customer–

it is important to tap into these life changing situations on an emotional basis. This will strengthen your awareness of the creative process.

In advertising, the Big Idea is the focus . . . taking a seemingly complex issue and creating something very special . . . by breaking down the parts into simple, clear and concise communication.

In life, as in business, creativity is spawned in making those complex issues simple. I became aware of this on an emotional level through the simple yet powerful insights of my small boys and their attitude toward others.

Sears became aware of simplicity in getting back to the basics of providing products their customer wanted and needed. Treating loved ones, peers, students and teachers, customers and managers on an emotional basis, and using a simple, emotional approach with each other begins to bring creativity to life. The unbridled, youthful approach to capturing the big idea is the topic of the next several chapters.

CHAPTER 6

MOLLY

When I was a boy, I knew a family of eight siblings. The sister, Molly, was subjected to all sorts of pressure being the only girl among the seven boys. Molly and her brothers were all very popular, athletic and the boys had a great sense of humor. I really enjoyed our friendship.

She was teased and ridiculed just like she was one of the boys . . . .and in her own way she was funny, charming and very kind. Because of her exposure to non-stop ribbing from her brothers, she grew outwardly self doubting.

Molly went to my high school and it was there that the years of "brotherly love" manifested itself in her. Although she was cute, her self-doubt precluded her from having self assurance. She was academically smart, yet she tended to put herself down. When she became interested in boys, Molly would approach a prospect and the situation in this fashion: *Hi. I know you don't think I am cute. And I know you don't like my friends . . . and you don't think I am smart and you would rather not . . . .but will you go out with me?*

Well, as you can guess, the prospective suitor would inevitably say "No" . . . .because he would be put in a position to agree with Molly. I embellish this story each time I tell it. However, think about the dynamics of this relationship. Molly, although attractive, smart, likeable and funny would paint a picture to inhibit those relationships she wanted.

In business we have to sometimes force clients to share with their customers their unique characteristics which make them stand out from their competitors. Perhaps it is embarrassing for them to tout the great things about their company. However, sharing with the public the history, the products and services

and your list may contain dozens or even hundreds of descriptors.

Establishing for yourself an objective inventory of your strengths and weaknesses, your positive and negative PQTs descriptors is important.

This process is done in business everyday. A SWOT analysis examines the strengths, weaknesses, opportunities and threats to an organization. By taking an inventory of the good and not so good qualities of an organization, a plan can be developed and implemented to correct any flaws and focus the energy of the company on a positive course of action.

One of our clients came to us with an unusual situation. They were a golf facility and country club that had a sixty year history. The previous owners of the club had been the only other owners since opening. The on site management was poor and membership had aged and dwindled. The owners had long since quit putting money back into the facility. Age and use had taken its toll, and the course's public image was very poor. Quite frankly, the club did not have a lot of positives.

The new owners began a two year process of turning the club around. Through on-site, daily management they began to make immediate physical changes and upgrades which were exciting to the existing members. They changed the membership requirements from private to semi-private which at first was a concern for some of the longtime members. Young families were also included as prospects for membership.

They engaged our agency and we began running newspaper ads each week inviting outside play. The dining room was remodeled and through advertising we began to invite the public to experience "something old, yet something new." The course was not a five star resort property, but it was a very comfortable property with a rich history that had a lot to offer prospective members. Our job was to tell them about the benefits.

In working with the client, we developed a list of positive qualities we wanted to highlight. Some of these qualities included: a rich history, former site of the local PGA championship tournament, a challenging course yet not "target golf" so much the rage, a traditional setting that was comfortable for seniors and young families, a reasonable price, great views, friendly atmosphere and more. In making the lists, we also addressed negatives including poor public image, intense upscale competition, dwindling and aging membership base and distant location.

The list of qualities is adjusted as changes take place as the owners invest back into the property. In the first year, the new owners invested millions into upgrades, the new management doubled the membership base, and through aggressive advertising and public relations we began to change the image of the facility in the marketplace. In just twelve short months, the country club became profitable and claimed "club of the year" and "general manager of the year" honors.

Now just making lists does not guarantee this kind of success. But understanding where the customer "ranks" your company in their mind and adjusting the challenges and opportunities to positive attributes can be a first and important step to success.

Taking an inventory for yourself about you is also important. You might try to isolate your PQT descriptors by yourself. I ask students to list their PQT in relation to their studies as part of their grading system, and we charge them with doing the same for me as professor. It is very interesting to take this inventory at the beginning and again at the end of the semester. You may want to ask someone you care about to make a list about you too.

CREATIVE BENCHMARK

Make a list of ten positive and ten negative PQT descriptors of yourself. Be objective and honest with yourself.

Your list should contain ten of each:

POSITIVE PQT   NEGATIVE PQT

_____ _____

_____ _____

_____ _____

_____ _____

_____ _____

_____ _____

_____ _____

_____ _____

_____ _____

_____ _____

This list will change with time, and upon reflection you may want to list more. Examine your PQT profile. On the Positive PQT side you have listed at least ten descriptors that you see as favorable. Some of these might be learned skills and others could be just part of your make-up. In Positive PQTs you will find the foundation of why YOU CAN be creative, because you have strengths which readily surface. These Positive PQTs can launch you in a creative direction.

Your Negative PQT list may show you some apparent flaws in your personality. However, if you change your paradigm, these same negative attributes could be actually positive. For example, if your Negative PQT lists "selfish" as an item, you could change the paradigm and work towards "frugality with charity". This takes a seemingly negative quality and makes it positive. If you wrote down "lazy" you could change the paradigm to reflect "conserver of energy for the important things in life".

Now I am stretching the point perhaps, but this exercise should start you thinking about your QUALITIES and how you can use your boundless gifts in productive and meaningful ways.

Molly turned out to be a very well qualified teacher, very well liked and very professional. She started with a good solid foundation and has parlayed that into something very special. Her brothers have also excelled in the marketplace.

Sometimes it is hard to boast about the positive qualities we possess. Whether that be on a resume, or in the first few months of a new relationship with someone special, or in a new client/customer setting. Telling why you are so great is hard at times.

But telling the positive qualities, these PQTs, are what people want to know. It is innate in us to be associated with winners or successful people. Our customers are the same way. Just like the golf course, the existing members became excited and the new members thought the facility was great. The positive energy was very refreshing.

Your positive PQT descriptors house your current creativity foundations . . . and your negative PQTs are important as well. Change the paradigm, the perspective you and your loved one or customers see as negative, and turn them into opportunities and creativity will explode from this.

LISTEN. It is how you look at yourself that is reflected in how others see you. In the next chapter, we will outline a way to be proactive about yourself.

On a regular basis, I return to that portfolio to review the good things about my academic career. The letters of recommendation from people whom I respect, the samples of my work and the whole feel of what I have accomplished are very important to keeping me centered and focused on my goals.

At my advertising agency, I have a file cabinet next to my desk. It contains all the current files for clients, teaching, and other important papers. One of the files is labeled *"feel good notes"*. In this file I keep all the thank you notes from students and clients, congratulatory letters and any correspondence which tells me the "good things" I do and have done. It also includes pictures my sons have drawn for me and other mementos. Occasionally, I look through this file to get energized and to again connect with my goals.

Peter Drucker, the great leadership guru, was one of the first scholars to suggest the use of a the mission statement to focus energy on the essentials of an organization. To him, the mission statement was a synthesis of the organization's "big idea" or their philosophy for being. The mission statement is a flexible yet steadfast way for organizations to achieve their goals.

In the world of marketing, we approach this through the concept of IMC, Integrated Marketing Communications.

My company has a mission statement. My father, who spent twenty-five years as a radio station manager, started our agency in 1968 with my mother. In the forties, fifties and sixties, they together managed radio stations in the west then settled in Tucson.

My mother often tells the story about their arrival to the Old Pueblo. They had come from Alliance, Nebraska where several of my brothers and sisters were born and as they came over the hill into the Tucson valley . . . my mother exclaimed that "this is it . . . we're not moving again!" It probably had something to do with a thousand plus mile trip being in a station wagon with all of my siblings and at the time she was pregnant with me!

After managing radio stations in Tucson my father became an entrepreneur and created Ackerley Advertising. The agency was small and family oriented with most of my brothers and sisters spending some time working there during their college years. Although I have had a few jobs including teaching,

we will earn the respect of our clients
and all those with whom we do business, and will be
recognized as a leader in the
advertising industry.

ACKERLEY ADVERTISING

Our company enjoys an outstanding reputation among our clients, the media and the community. I attribute this to the legacy that my parents have brought to the company and reflects their work ethic, honesty and living by the golden rule. Our company's integrity and reputation supercedes the creative product, even our professional expertise and personal relationships as the most important "product" that we offer our clients. The simple mission statement has helped us keep our goals in focus and has guided us in the success of our agency.

Vision statements are a lot like dieting or preparing for a marathon. Like creativity, visions statements do not come overnight but are the result of process. There is no magic wand that can be waived to get us to our dream. It usually takes practice, hard work and tenacity.

radio disc jockey and youth minister . . . all the w
I have been at the agency. My training in the busir
has come about because of my first hand exposur
client service, new business development and mana
ment consulting at our company. A couple of years ;
we developed a mission statement to help guide us i
the new century. Here it is:

MISSION STATEMENT

At Ackerley Advertising,
our mission is to provide quality advertising
and marketing services to our clients
at reasonable prices and on a timely basis.
Working as an effective team,
our desire is to create and produce result-oriented
advertising campaigns for each of our clients
to help them grow their business . . .
because we know that their success
will help insure our success.
We believe in maintaining the highest levels
of professional ethics and personal integrity.
We also believe in actively supporting our community
through involvement in selected public service campaigns.
Our goal is to operate a successful business,
meeting all our obligations,
and earning a reasonable profit for our efforts.
As a result of fulfilling these commitments,

Keep positive influence in your life handy, whether you keep a file of "feel good notes" or photographs on the wall. I have three voice mail messages on my phone that I saved over two years ago. I listen to them now and again when I need a lift (two are from my boys and one from someone who had hired me for a seminar).

A company needs a mission statement, just like an individual needs a vision. Operating a business without a mission statement is akin to traveling in a foreign land without a map . . . you can get to your goal but it may take a lot of energy, frustration and disappointment. Having a mission provides the shortest route to success if it is realistic and within the realm of possibilities. Businesses that focus on the Integrated Marketing Communications Process, devoting one-hundred percent of their energy to achieving their goal, tend to be the most successful.

Achieving a goal through the vision statement process is something that starts everyday. Step by step, becoming more creative is something you have to work on each and every day. It is simple, but it just will not happen. Write down your vision for your life, and include "to become more creative". Do it, and you will.

meeting with the founder and principal and express our concerns about the way Kevin's teacher was viewing him. Or I could get angry and make a scene. Or request a new teacher. The "problem" with Kevin as I saw it was not that he was behaving poorly, but that his social skills were not at the same level as his academics. And those that were working with him expected him to act like the nine and ten year olds in his group. I had to "change the paradigm." I went to my advertising agency and created a post card. You see, with a post card, anyone who handles the mail will see the card. The card was addressed to Kevin. On one side there was a huge "Congratulations Kevin Ackerley". On the other side a short message from mom and dad, his brothers and our dog:

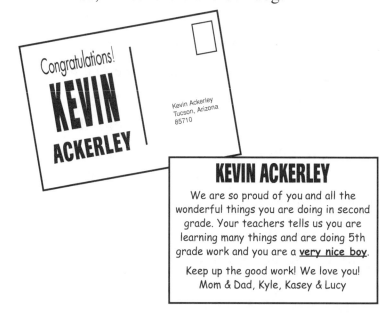

KEVIN ACKERLEY

We are so proud of you and all the wonderful things you are doing in second grade. Your teachers tells us you are learning many things and are doing 5th grade work and you are a **very nice boy**.

Keep up the good work! We love you!
Mom & Dad, Kyle, Kasey & Lucy

I mailed the postcard to the school . . . .and it wound up in the principal's mail . . . and she hand delivered the card to Kevin's class and the teacher and Kevin read the card together. There was an instant paradigm shift . . . ..those in charge of our son's academic life realized <u>he was a nice boy</u> . . . he was just six years old and acting like it.

Needless to say, the postcard from home changed an important perspective and Kevin has never looked back.

In my classes at the university, I tell this story each semester. I also talk about the tendency in our current culture to use technology to communicate. Most of my students do their work via computer, are connected to the internet and have cell phones and pagers. Most of my contact out of the classroom is via e-mail and voice mail. As we discuss in class the professional decorum they should develop I ask them a simple question . . . when was the last time you wrote a hand-written thank you note? Most of the time, none of them can answer with confidence because hand writing anything anymore seems a lost art. The majority of the students forge on through their life and communicate via email or voice mail and have in effect lost the power of human communication.

I point this out because the human connection we make in our lives can be a driving force of creativity. The professional act of writing a thank you note is important, but even more important to learning the art of interpersonal communication.

Thank you notes are a good example of this concept, because when a person writes a thank you note they usually are thanking someone for something specific, i.e. a gift, or a great time, or an act of kindness and a special thought. The return thank you note is focusing on one item that has made a difference in someone's life.

In this day and age of total technological connectedness, I would argue the art of interpersonal communication has been lost. It is easy to sit at a computer and craft long and wordy messages.

I often get emails that start and end with no frame of reference, many times because the person is simply responding to a previous email. This lack of a frame of reference becomes comical at times as you read a message that someone has sent by hitting "reply" and just answering a message like it is a conversation.

The focus of interpersonal communication is to connect with the very emotion and human contact we talked about earlier. Creative communication is that which is focused, clear and simple. Take for instance a business letter. I am of the feeling if one ever writes a business letter of more than one page, they really do not have a lot to say. A powerful letter is one which says more with less words and creates a dynamic where the reader has to read and has to respond.

CREATIVE BENCHMARK

Hand write a personal thank you note. (You can easily purchase a pack of thank you notes from a local retail store . . . keep them handy and use them). The note should be to someone who has made a "difference" in your life . . . .a spouse, child, parent, friend, mentor, co-worker, teacher, boss . . . and thank them for something specific they have done for you. This personal thank you note will have a dramatic effect, especially if you thank someone from your past with whom you have not communicated lately. Make the note short and to the point, and make it genuine.

The purpose of this exercise is to get you to think about the human connections in your life and how important this specific relationship is to you as a person. And this should be the stepping stone to you writing more thank you notes, postcards, and hand-written letters to those you respect and love . . . .because creative communication from the heart, with emotion and feeling, are some one of the best ways to nurture the human condition.

As a business skill, learning how to write effectively is imperative for success. The power of a positive letter (or a negative slant) can be the difference for success. Take for instance accounts receivable. Sometimes it is difficult to 'ask for money' from clients and customers. Often, I witness my clients having trouble making the ask and I myself have had a hard time with this. This is partly due to the self doubt we sometimes possess.

Over the years, we have found that writing a succinct, simple and clear letter to our clients who owe us money results in quick and deliberate action. The wording of our letter is simple and usually looks like this: *your company owes money on your advertising bill and the media should be paid in a timely fashion. Your immediate attention to this matter would be appreciated.*

This is also effective when you simply call and deliver the same short communication! You would be surprised how general managers and bookkeepers react to the simple message that they owe us money. But, to be fair, when past due bills are paid we send a THANK YOU NOTE acknowledging the payment!

Sometimes, creativity means analyzing a practical situation and brainstorming solutions. Much like I did with my child's second grade teachers, I had to come up to something that would change the paradigm.

As technology advances, I propose that you use human contact as often as possible to deliver a powerful message. In person would be great, but when that is not possible I suggest hand written thank you notes or short focussed letters. Think about the difference between your frame of mind when 'responding to emails' versus what you do when you sit down and write a personal letter (have you written a letter lately?) When you respond to email you are acting machine-like in your response . . . when you write a letter you are acting human like and thinking about how the reader will respond to your words.

So take the time to make communication personal, unexpected and powerful. Try not to rely on technology to deliver your message, deliver a powerful message through technology. Focused. Clear. Simple.

Understanding how powerful communication can be will help you understand how creativity can enhance your human relationships.

CHAPTER 9

LOOK IN FROM OUTSIDE

When I was a young man, I played volleyball. This sport is enjoyable because it is like soccer, most anyone can play it regardless of their ability. The strategy is very simple, as a team of six with three hits of the ball, make the ball go over the net to land in the opponent's court. The game is fun, fast and exciting.

I also became a referee as part of my exposure to the game. This gave me the opportunity of being an official at upper level, very fast and powerful men's AAA volleyball. These guys were amazing. They were strong, fast and worked well together as a team. They knew each other's strengths and weaknesses and worked them to the team's advantage.

As it is with men, most of them had mastered the skills of the game and knew the rules of the game from their years of play. That meant that each of them were well versed in the intricate rules and regulations of the game, many of which are "objective" (more than three hits, illegal rotation, etc.) However, many of the rules and officiating are "subjective" (i,e, touching the net, in or out, illegal hit, etc). Rarely were the objective calls challenged, but more often than not my subjective calls would be criticized by the offending team.

In volleyball officiating you keep control in several ways. The official has a whistle which starts and stops play. The official stands on a platform for a better view of the court and only addresses the captain of each team when interpreting a rule or instructing. The official uses a yellow card (warning) and red card (point/side out or ejection) which without talking to the offender can be flashed and indicate there will be no more discussion . . . the official has made a ruling.

On one painful occasion, I had the duty of officiating a close men's championship game. The players on both sides were good, very good, many of them coaches themselves in high school.

I started the match and about halfway through the first game a player on one team began to criticize my calls. This went on for a while so eventually I flashed the yellow card warning. That just made matters worse . . . .so eventually I flashed the red card. This gave the opposing team a point. Then the outburst became even more heated. I listened for a brief moment and tried to continue the game, but this individual (spurred on by his teammates) was very vocal and somewhat disrespectful. I had two options . . . to flash both cards and eject the player which would make matters worse . . . or change the paradigm. I chose the latter.

Play began again with my whistle . . . the ball was in play and the teams were working the ball. And this player was working his mouth . . . so without warning I descended the platform (during play) and walked onto the court right next to the offensive player.

I took my whistle off from around my neck and held it out to him and said, "if you think you are so good, you get up on the platform and officiate".

He was stunned! He was also speechless. I glared at him for what seemed a minute and there was dead silence on the court. He said nothing, I returned to the platform and for the remainder of the match he said nothing and later came up and apologized.

In one of my first semesters as a teacher at the University of Arizona I was giving a lecture when a student raised her hand and began asking questions about my grading system. She had turned in an assignment and she was criticizing the grade she received. I explained that I would talk with her after class, but she continued to complain about the grade.

I suggested a five minute break, and she came up to me and I said that an appointment was in order and we could arrange this after class. When the students all returned, this same student raised her hand and began complaining again about the grade she received. I tried to dissuade her from continuing, however this just fueled her emotions and her girlfriend sitting next to her also began to make comments. They were both loud and disruptive. I suggested another five minute break because by this time I was getting upset too.

When the students returned a second time, the two continued their complaining. Another student stood up and remarked that this was the best class he had ever taken, and although he respected their right to complain, this simply was not the place or time to harass the professor. They continued!

I knew I needed to change the paradigm, and do it quickly. I opened my briefcase and put my lecture notes, textbook and gradesheet inside, closed it and walked out of the room!

The next morning I called my department chair and related the situation. She supported my decision but indicated you "only do this once or twice in your teaching career"..and she related a similar story from her own experience. Incidentally, the two students were required to apologize in writing to me, to the chair and sign a behavior contract in order to return to the class two weeks later. These two students did not receive the grade they expected, and I changed their point of view.

LISTEN: Sometimes you have to do drastic things to change the paradigm. There are occasions when you simply have to take charge and help others see things from a different perspective.

Many times in my seminars I hold up my hands to form a small "window". I look through this window suggesting this is how most people see their life, and their life's situation. And then holding my hands out, I turn them slightly to "change the view".

After changing the view, I move my body into position so that I can look back through the window. What a difference! You can make small changes in the way you look through your window, and this will definitely enhance your life. But sometimes, in an important relationship, in a marriage, in a business deal, student-teacher relationship . . . you may need to look into the other person's window to see things differently, from their point of view.

In advertising this is our constant challenge. To see from the viewpoint of the viewer, the listener or reader. And this principle is important for you too, whether you are crafting a thank you note, a letter, or simply talking with someone . . . looking through their window will enhance your communication and will help you relate dramatically with them.

CREATIVE BENCHMARK

The next time you are at your desk or computer and you hit a block and seem to not be able to continue, stand up. Get out of your chair and work for five or ten minutes standing. This is a simple but very effective way to prioritize your work and helps you put your tasks in perspective. It works. Try it! In business, it is important to look through the window that the customer views you as a company. This is at times very difficult to do.

Many companies employ consultants to help get a fresh perspective on how the customer sees things. I had the occasion to serve one of our clients by conducting a "mystery shopping" experience to test their customer service. The venue was a hotel in a resort community which was privately owned.

When I first arrived on the property I was not impressed with the physical layout of the hotel and its apparent age. This negative feeling stayed with me through the check-in process as the service was less than adequate. My drive around the property confirmed my instinct that the hotel was dated. The parking in the back of the property, the walk up the stairs (which were filthy as was the outdoor carpets leading to the room) and the door to my room was weathered and discolored. However, walking into the room this negative feeling went away as the room was bright and colorful.

At check in, although I had #207 reserved and it was printed right on my registration/reservation material, the attendant searched and said "we only have one room remaining, let me see if I can get it for you". The SAME room as on my registration/ reservation. He was very unsure. No name tag. He looked "disheveled" and his pants were unzipped part-way.

My first impression of the hotel was "Oh my gosh, what have I got myself into?" It was old look-ing, the help up front was terrible. I was not looking forward to being here. But it got worse!

That evening I dined in the hotel restaurant. The hostess was pleasant but firm. She seemed outwardly stern and she greeted with some vibrancy. The overall ambiance of the restaurant was bright and cheerful. However, the restaurant showed some signs of age.

When I first was seated there was music play-ing on the sound system. It was much too loud for the amount of people in the restaurant. Later a guitarist began to play . . . and during his breaks he was loud when he talked . . . and spoke loudly to the staff about trivial things. There was a tremendous amount of small talk among the employees. The entertainer tried to "engage" the guests who were enjoying quiet dinners by saying things to capture their attention. He embar-rassed me in front of the guests when he singled me out and made a comment about me. On a scale of 1-10, the food quality was about a "4" and the whole experience about a "5". Definitely NOT worth the price.

Friday evening after dinner, I went down to the lobby and the attendant was seated around the corner watching TV. A young woman about twenty five, I had earlier seen her in the restaurant talking with the host-ess and the guitarist.

She did not have on a uniform, and she stood up in front of the television. I asked if there were any good places to hike. She was somewhat puzzled, and replied that she did not really know..and then walked around the counter and gave me the piece of paper. She was not helpful, not knowledgeable, and it seemed like I had interrupted her TV program and that she was a little annoyed. She was really no help at all. Upon checkout on Saturday morning, I walked into the lobby. Behind the counter there was a young woman and a man engaged in conversation. She was telling him about how a (former) boss treated her. He was listening, and asking questions and she went on and on. As I approached the counter, he simply said "CHECK OUT?" . . . .. he went to the computer and continued the conversation with the woman, and never spoke to me again!

He never asked how my stay was, never engaged me with any conversation, yet the two of them continued to talk the entire time I was standing at the counter.

I was amazed. In all the years of consulting with clients this was by far the worst customer service I had experienced. If only, if only I could convey this to the property owner I think they too would be amazed. It is incredible to me that employees would sink to the level of inept service as these demonstrated.

Many of the negatives could have been turned into positives. The "oldness" of the hotel could be translated into "quaintness with history". The rooms were modern and the atmosphere was comfortable. There were a lot of pluses to the hotel. But looking at the property through the "window" of a customer gave a different perspective.

This is an actual case study and "mystery shopping" consulting experience. And as a result of this service there were dramatic changes in staff. If you are ever in the position of delivering service, it is always good to get a renewed and refreshed perspective on a regular basis. I like to work at any new client's place of business for a day to really understand their goals and objectives.

Sometimes you have to dramatically change the paradigm to effect a change in perspective. Much like handing the whistle to the volleyball player, closing the briefcase and leaving, or having someone act like a customer and give an unbiased viewpoint . . . it is important to "walk a mile in the customer's shoes" so this perspective can be realized.

You can do this in your personal relationships too. Spend a day at your child's school, or your spouse's place of work, or spend some time with a loved one in their own setting, and soon you will understand the power of "looking through a different window".

This ability to see things from a different perspective is a very important fundamental in honing your creative skills.

CHAPTER 10

CREATIVITY BEGINS AT HOME

During a recent lunch in an interchange between several hotel directors of marketing, the topic arose of how to deal with the "gas crisis" during the summer. The high temperatures make these months difficult. Add a gas crisis to this time of year and there was a lot of concern expressed by the hotel marketing directors. How were they going to attract local leisure guests when gas prices could be thirty to fifty percent higher than the previous summer?

After listening to the discussion for a few minutes I suggested they embrace the problem rather than be concerned about it. So I recommended they change their perspective and promote a free tank of gas for weekend getaway packages.

After the meeting, one of the questions was "how do you think like that?" I often receive comments from people about the way I think "so creatively" and they wonder how I do it. To answer the question, I will tell you a story.

On Labor Day weekend my family was sitting around our house. It was hot, but we all wanted to do something. So we decided to play "the choosing game". We took a piece of paper and tore it into equal parts. Each member of the family wrote down an idea and my wife helped our youngest with his idea.

All of us participated. We placed the ideas into a bowl and agreed that whatever was pulled out we would do. After we drew the winner I examined the other ideas. They were "go to the park and swing", "movie", "swimming" and other family outings. However, in a few short minutes we were packed and on our way to the beach in southern California.

On another occasion, my wife came into our room and woke me up at about midnight. She said "wake up, let's go." She had packed the car, had the boys asleep inside and I was the last one to be loaded. When the boys awoke in the morning, our oldest asked where we were. And in a few short minutes we pulled into the parking lot of Disneyland . . . much to the delight of three small boys! Now, I am not suggesting that you have to take a road trip to be creative. However, spontaneity does help, Creativity begins at home!

This is an extremely important point. You spend the majority of your leisure time, by definition, at your home. It is there that the critical concepts of creativity are born, and it is there where you can learn some valuable lessons. Take for instance, a spouse. I often tell my audiences, especially young students at the university, that the hardest thing I have ever had to do is to be married. Now, do not get me wrong. I love my wife and my life and being married is a glorious experience. However, each and everyday I have to tell myself "what am I going to do to honor Susie?" By honoring, I mean what things can I do in my life to show her how important she is to me?

In our life, like most parents, our children provide a convenient vehicle for this. I often remark that when I was single I played a lot of golf, did my share of happy hours, and took a lot of trips. When I was first married, although I modified these habits, it took a while for commitment and responsibility to set in as a newlywed. It was not until I felt the awesome challenge of fatherhood that I totally committed myself to our family.

I think we are all like that to some extent, when our children come into our lives we suddenly feel one of the most powerful forces. To have my young sons look up at me in awe, almost daily, is a very rewarding thing about parenthood.

The best way I can honor our family is to honor my wife and children everyday.

I am forever impressed at how my wife schedules our boys time, diligently planning their next activity whether it be sports, swimming, baseball, piano, football, chorus, basketball, chess, soccer, creative writing, (did I mention sports)? I often call her van "Susie's taxi". She is everywhere with those boys and I often feel she has as much fun as they do. During the summer each year she conducts "Camp Ackerley" where she takes our guys to the various attractions, national forests, the libraries, galleries and other places to learn and grow. We often say that thousands of people come to our city each year to visit . . . so we want to make sure our boys know why.

As both of us have education degrees, one of the areas we feel is vital for our children is education. That is why we have invested in private education. Not that we are against public education, but in our particular situation we have found that private education during their formative years works best for us. As a supplement to their formal education, my wife has tutored each of them in math and reading skills spending countless hours with each of them reinforcing the basics.

As a kindergarten teacher herself, Susie knows how important a solid base is for learning. That is why both she and I devote about an hour each night to read to the boys. There are numerous studies that show that reading to your children when they are young can be the difference for their education, and we take this responsibility seriously.

We do many things in our family to be creative and to make memories for our children. Take a case in point of our youngest son Kasey. He is a "new age hiker" . . . he absolutely loves to go exploring in the forest. One of his most treasured items is to find a perfect stick that he and I can carve into a walking stick.

On a recent trip to southern California we had loads of action figures, toys and sticks! Why all these sticks? Kasey simply loves to hike and he likes to take his walking sticks with him. (His hunting of the perfect stick reminds me of me and alley hopping).

Kevin is our star athlete. As a young boy he was extremely coordinated, fast and strong for his age. And he simply loves to play anything that has to do with a ball. Kevin can shoot baskets for literal hours on end and still want to play some more when we call him. He will swing forever, loves to swim laps and be 'timed' as he races himself, and simply loves sports. One day I picked him up from school and told him we were going to a big game . . . .and he wanted to know where. I told him he would just be watching a game and as we drove we talked about why he like sports so much. This was a surprise for Kevin and dad. When we arrived at the game he was so excited, he wanted as many souvenirs as he could carry. Watching the Phoenix Suns play was a great treat for him and driving ninety minutes back to Tucson he talked non-stop about sports and how someday he too might be a star.

Our eldest son Kyle is our performer. A star in his own right with the Tucson Arizona Boys Chorus, he has a talent for acting and singing. A gifted student he receives high marks at school and as an athlete he does well in swimming, running and other sports. In his young life as a chorister he has performed in Mexico, Canada, China, Venezuela, Chile plus travelling throughout the United States. Kyle has the gift of performance. My wife an I have done what we can to encourage this gift he has. He is a talented pianist, singer and musician including the drums! He has spent countless hours playing (playing, and playing!) those drums.

For all three of our boys, we go well beyond what we should to provide for them a nurturing environment. We owe much of this to Susie, who believes, as do I, that the very best for our sons is that which will help them succeed in the future. As precious gifts, we only have them in our charge for a few short years and we want to make sure we provide for them the most rewarding of years.

It is perhaps in nature that we have been most creative. Our sons have been to the mountain tops, the canyons, deserts and oceans . . . to the east coast and west coast . . . and on each of these trips we take time to walk and discover. Our boys spend hours searching for the perfect rock, just the right stick, that precious leaf or searching for life in a pool of water.

Lucy and Buddy are our Golden Retrievers. When Lucy was having our puppies, we all stayed home from school (and work) to witness the blessed event as ten little puppies were born. Each of those puppies are now full grown and doing well, probably because of the hundreds of hugs, kisses and cuddles they received during their first few months of life. My children respect life and their lives as a result of the creative way in which we have shown them the power of nature and the simple things.

CREATIVE BENCHMARK

Creativity begins at home. These are just a few examples from my own personal family. You should create similar special moments with family. To be creative within your own family can help you bring creativity to all aspects of your life. Try some of these tricks: Instead of watching television one night, lay down on the ground and watch the unfolding universe of the night sky. Instead of rushing through a meal, pack up the family for a picnic in a local park. Make a nice meal, pack it up in your car, and drive to someone's house and surprise them. Go to the mall, but not to shop, simply sit and watch people. Take a walk around your neighborhood and discover things and people you perhaps have driven by a thousand times, but never stopped to look or to talk to them.

You can enhance your life in your business as well. My office is in a large building with a myriad of people working in medical offices and real estate.

Everyday, dozens of people walk within ten feet of me coming and going about their busy day. They retreat into the confines of their "cubicle". None of them has ever come into my office to see what I do, to meet our staff or become friendly.

So, at the annual holiday party for the complex, it was me that was engaging many of them in conversation, asking them what they did and how they made their living. What a different perspective I now have of this "building" and the people who work here each day.

My schedule as an advertising agency principal, husband, father, university professor, consultant and civic leader leaves little time 'just for me'. But within the confines of these roles I play, engaging new people helps enrich my perspective on creativity. You can do this too, and it will enrich your life as well.

CREATIVE BENCHMARK:

Read a story as a family, each taking turns to read. If the little ones need help, help them, but in such a way that they too have a special moment. Sing songs as a family, even if you are not the best musicians. Just singing can really bring a family together. Have a campout with mom and dad and all the kids. Taking the time to make some special memories as a family can be extremely rewarding. And remember, quality not quantity. It is the quality of the creative experience you will all remember. And be sure to include everyone in the decision making process so that all feel part of the fun. Bring some creativity into your life at home and you will reap huge benefits in other areas of your life.

In your business, call a competitor! Talk with them about the problems they face and how they cope. Ask them for the good ideas they have discovered which have helped them. Talk to your customers. Invite a customer out to lunch to talk with them about how they see your company. Share your vision statement with these good customers and ask them if you are living up to it.

Rearrange the furniture in your office to give you freedom to move, to be interactive with others and to feel more energy in the workspace.

It's about being aware of creativity. Take a new, clean look at your life at home and work and make creative adjustments and you will begin to see your creativity blossom.

CHAPTER 11

FIRST CLASS

On a recent trip home I was delayed for an hour in the airport. Like the majority of the passengers, I was patient and waited for instructions. I was standing in line at the gate to insure I had a seat and a man and his wife were in front of me was at the counter. He was very upset and rude to the employees of the airline. He was also loud, and his obnoxious demeanor was really noticeable to those in the area.

The clerks were checking people in, and one supervisor was handling this disgruntled passenger. He demanded a first class seat because of the delay and was getting belligerent. She completed his ticketing and he had a few choice words to the supervisor and he and his wife left the counter. I was next and I approached the counter and asked her calmly, "how long have you been working with the airline?"

She said she had been there for several years. Then I remarked, "this job of yours would be great if you didn't have to put up with customers". She laughed and we continued to have a pleasant talk as she processed my ticket. We had a conversation about the airline, about her job and I asked her about the Marketing Vice-President of the airline whom I knew. Although she did not personally know him, we continued to chat as if we were old friends.

As I boarded the plane, I took my seat and the disgruntled passenger and his wife passed me as I drank my drink in first class and they were headed for the coach section!

On a a trip to South Dakota I was dropped off at the airport after making a speech and walked into the terminal. As the airport was relatively small, I was the only person in line to get my seat because I was about two hours early for my flight. Per custom, I began a conversation with the ticket agent. We talked about Tucson and the "dry heat" . . . her visits there and why

I was in Rapid City. I talked with her about Creating-Magic and what a powerful force creativity is. At the end of the conversation, she simply asked where I would you like to sit. I responded "first class". She responded that I was a nice guy and indeed she put me into a first class seat.

Now the CEOs of these airline companies may not agree with putting just any person like me in first class seats, however, I share these stories with you to demonstrate a point. You can be creative in your approach to your life, and it can bring you instant rewards.

Indeed, it is the attitude with which you approach your life that counts. If you have been on line for any length of time, you most certainly have received your share of email jokes and stories. A friend sent this to me: Many years ago, when I worked as a volunteer at a local hospital, there was a story about a little girl named Jenna who was suffering from a rare and serious disease. Her only chance of recovery appeared to be a blood transfusion from her five year old brother, who had miraculously survived the same disease and had developed the antibodies, needed to combat the illness.

The doctor explained to her little brother, and asked the boy if he would be willing to give his blood to his sister. I saw him hesitate for a second only to say "Yes, I'll do it if it will save Jenna."

As the transfusion progressed, he lay in bed next to his sister and smiled, as we all did, seeing the color returning to her cheeks. Then his face grew pale and his smile faded. He looked up at the doctor and asked with a trembling voice, "Will I start to die right away?" Being young, the boy had misunderstood the doctor; he thought he was going to have to give his sister all of his blood. Attitude, after all, is everything. Attitude is important. This is part of my portfolio:

ATTITUDE IS EVERYTHING

Attitude is the way you think. Your attitude is something other people can actually see. They can hear it in your voice, see it in the way you move, feel it when they are with you. Your attitude expresses itself in everything you do, all the time, wherever you are. Positive attitudes always invite positive results. Negative attitudes always invite negative results. Attitude makes a difference every hour, every day, in everything that you do for your entire life. What you get out of each thing you do will equal the attitude you have when you do it. Anything you do with a positive attitude will work for you, anything with a negative attitude will work against you. If you have a positive attitude, you are looking for ways to solve the problems that you can solve. And you are letting go of the things over which you have no control. You can develop a positive attitude by emphasizing the good, by being tough-minded and by refusing defeat. **LISTEN**: *Creativity* is about attitude.

CREATIVE BENCHMARK:

Dip into your emotion. Take five minutes today and write a letter to someone significant in your life, this could be to a romantic letter to your spouse. Take the time to share with that person the reasons they are special to you, and share with them from your unique perspective their Personal Quality Traits (PQT) that make you want to be their friend or lover. Develop the interpersonal communication with this person over the next few months, with personal notes, leave letters on their car window, email them photos of you together, send them a postcard. Use interpersonal communication skills to enhance your life together. With just five minutes per day thinking about how you can enhance your relationship, you will enhance your life in ways you may never have imagined.

Pencil in your child for a working lunch at your favorite restaurant. Spend a day at your client's place of business to really see what it is they do.

When I was a young account executive, I spent many hours at my office. Sometimes I would be working in the office at midnight, or coming in early at 4a.m. to work on projects for clients. During this time, I met a graphic artist who also experienced this entrepreneurial approach to work, spending leisure time at the office to meet the deadlines imposed by his clients.

We discussed the trials of operating a small business and how we had sacrifice a lot to a keep our ambitious goals in perspective.

During this time, he and I both had taken other odd assignments to supplement our income. I was teacher, he photographed weddings at night. I did yardwork and paper routes, he helped young people with the look of their resumes.

Both of us had spent many hours, sacrificed a lot, and were feeling somewhat overwhelmed. He had been to a seminar on creativity and he came back with a suggestion he shared with me. Raise your rates! What, charge my clients MORE for the same service? No Way. That would be sure disaster and we would lose business. We did raise our rates and guess what happened? We lost clients. But we retained clients who had no problem investing in our expertise. We cut down our actual hours in the office, quit pulling all nighters and both of us began to make more!

Quality is an important part of creativity. In fact, in our agency motto we use four important words: Creativity, simplicity, clarity and *quality*. In business, there are customers who are willing to pay for first class ideas, first class executions and customer service. In these days of incredible schedules, time management, increased competition and choices, stress, pressure and demands . . . begin to demonstrate and adopt more quality and you will begin to be rewarded with creativity. Becoming more creative is about simplifying your life, looking for the big idea and recapturing the play of your youth. It is about clarifying your goals and vision, and articulating what you are trying to achieve. It is about making quality an important part of your personal relationships and your business activities.

CHAPTER 12

CREATING MAGIC

You can become more creative and use creativity to make your life magical. God only knows how desperately we need more creativity in our world. In Chapter 1 *Creativity* is described as best accomplished when we change our point of view. To see how you are doing with changing your point of view, try to answer these few questions:

How many outs are there in an inning?
Do they have 4th of July in England?
A butcher is six feet two inches tall, what
    does he weigh?

Of course the answers are six, yes just after the third and before the fifth, and meat. These simple questions give you a playful example of how to look at situations creatively. Hopefully you have caught onto the skill of looking at something from a different perspective. You will become more creative when you learn to look at life from the perspective of others, while maintaining your own vision and goals. One of the greatest tenets from all major religions is the Golden Rule . . . treat others as you wish to be treated . . . and in this regard creativity will be born.

Begin to strip away the limits imposed on you through habit and social conditioning. Unlock your inhibitions of a learned response of "coloring inside the lines." Understand the concept of simplicity.

Design a personal vision statement. Generate clarity in your life. Think. Find the Big Idea. Start now to understand interpersonal relationships. The magical power of creating something new . . . *Creativity* begins in our thoughts and ideas. You have the skill and power to enhance your life by unleashing your thoughts from a new perspective. Find the very treasures of your life which will spawn your creativity.

Step back to the playfulness of your youth and look forward in the most creative way you can. Give yourself time each day to ask the question "how can I enhance the life of those around me today?" In answering the question, and acting upon it, you will enhance your own life too.

Here is a little thought you can share:

Today, I will see your smiling face.

I will let you get dressed by yourself, whatever you choose to wear. At breakfast, you can eat whatever you want, even ice cream. We'll mess up your room together when we play. There will be no tv, computer, telephone or clocks. You can make popcorn and spill it all over the house. We'll order pizza for lunch. In the afternoon we'll take a nap together. Then you can take a bubble bath . . . with the dogs . . . and then we'll have a picnic for dinner out on the grass. Tonight we'll read ten books, and two of them again. And then we'll pray. I'll pray first, then you . . . then we'll pray together.

Then I will tell you how special you really are.

LISTEN. To enhance creativity in your own life you must become more childlike everyday have the courage and conviction to unleash your creative power.

As you become more aware of creativity, realize that the best creativity is that which is simple. Universally appealing. Emotional. Something beautiful . . . it helps to have a sense of humor. Spend five minutes everyday . . . making your life more CREATIVE. Take time to realize IT'S A WONDERFUL WORLD!

That's Creating**MAGIC**.

Chapter 13

NOT THE LAST WORD

When I began to research creativity, I was approached by an expert in leadership who argued that "creativity" is a gift, something that cannot be learned. Obviously, I strongly disagree. I feel that you can become more creative through the awesome power of our ability to THINK, and in this we can be and do anything we want. Our humanness allows us the opportunity to be creative simply by developing the habits of "thinking" and using creativity as a daily viewpoint. This looking through another window, changing the paradigm and seeking out the good in others really is important. After I gave a presentation, I received this:

One day an expert in time management was speaking to a group of business students and used an illustration those students will never forget. As he stood in front of the group of high powered over achievers he said, "Okay, time for a quiz." He then proceeded to produce a one-gallon, wide mouthed Mason jar and set it on the table in front of him. Then he produced about a dozen fist-sized rocks and carefully placed them, one at a time, into the jar. When the jar was filled to the top and no more rocks would fit inside, he asked, "Is this jar full?" Everyone in the class said, "Yes." Then he said, "Really?" He reached under the table and pulled out a bucket of gravel. Then he dumped some gravel in and shook the jar causing pieces of gravel to work themselves down into the space between the big rocks. Then he asked the group once more, "Is the jar full?" By this time the class was on to him. "Probably not," one of them answered. "Good!" he replied. He reached under the table and brought out a bucket of sand. He started dumping the sand in the jar and it went into all of the spaces left between the rocks and the gravel. Once more he asked the question, "Is this jar full?" "No!" the class shouted. Once again he said, "Good." Then he grabbed a pitcher of water and began to pour it in until the jar was filled to the brim.

Then he looked at the class and asked, "What is the point of this illustration?" One eager beaver raised his hand and said, "The point is, no matter how full your schedule is, if you try really hard you can always fit some more things in it!"

"No," the teacher replied, "that's not the point. The truth this illustration teaches us is: If you don't put the big rocks in first, you'll never get them in at all."

What are the 'big rocks' in your life? Your children, your loved ones, your education, your dreams, a worthy cause, teaching, mentoring others, doing things that you love, time for yourself, your health, your significant other? Remember to put these BIG ROCKS in first or you'll never get them in at all. If you sweat the little stuff (the gravel, the sand) then you'll fill your life with little things you worry about that don't really matter, and you'll never have the real quality time you need to spend on the big, important stuff (the big rocks).

Much more study can be done to show how creativity can enhance our lives. However, if we begin to strive for excellence, with a creative approach – you will see magic happen.

Change your own viewpoint. Change the paradigm of your life. Begin to break the rules. Focus on the child within you. Become more childlike in your approach to creativity. Notice the small things and appreciate nature. Tap into your emotions. Adopt a simple view of complex issues and break down these concepts into new ideas. Put two previously discarded ideas together and build something new. Look through your customer's window when you look at your business.

You can enhance your personal life, your interpersonal relationships and use creativity to advance your career, to achieve your goals, your dreams and aspirations. Then you will know the true meaning of Creating**MAGIC**!

About the **AUTHOR**

ED ACKERLEY, M.Ed. and his wife Susan E. Ackerley, M.Ed. have three boys, Kyle, Kevin and Kasey and live in Tucson, Arizona.

Ed Ackerley is a principal at Ackerley Advertising in Tucson. The company was created in 1968 by Ed's parents, Gene and Gloria Ackerley and his brothers Keating, Julian and William and his sister Ande all worked at the company while attending college. Gene, Gloria, Bill and Ed remain at the agency and specialize in advertising for retailers, hotels, golf courses and tourism accounts.

Ed Ackerley is a graduate of the University of Arizona and Northern Arizona University, where he is an adjunct instructor at both schools. He is a Past Chairman of the Council of Governors of the American Advertising Federation and Past President of the Tucson Advertising Federation and was named Tucson's Advertising Professional of the Year in 1988 and to the Tucson Advertising Federation Hall Of Fame in 1989. In 1999, he was awarded the prestigious American Advertising Federation Silver Medal Award to recognize his outstanding lifelong contributions to advertising and creative excellence.

For information on Creating**MAGIC** keynote speeches and seminars:
PHONE: 520.850.7058
EMAIL: Doctor**MAGIC**27622@aol.com

NOTES

NOTES

NOTES